Hello! Welcome to the third Our Favourite Places (OFP) book – an independent guide to the best of Sheffield.

OFP is a celebration of our home city – a snapshot of places that we love, places that do things a little differently.

Sheffield can be a pretty modest city, and our book reflects that. Some of its very best places are not in the least bit showy; you could easily pass by some of the best restaurants without noticing them, or overlook whole areas of the city that, beneath the surface, are bursting with charm. That's where we come in.

We want you to experience Sheffield's warmth and character, to scratch the surface of our unconventionally beautiful city, and to enjoy the kind of places that only locals know about.

OFP isn't an exhaustive guide to Sheffield, but we reckon there's something to excite or inspire any visitor to the city – whether you're here for an afternoon or a long weekend; whether you're new to Sheffield or an old friend of the city.

You'll find more on our website – including our guide to what's on in the city, tips and pointers to get you exploring, and our online shop filled with prints and tours. Enjoy!

ourfaveplaces.co.uk

◆

Our Favourite Places is a self-initiated project by Eleven, a creative design studio based in Sheffield. It is our love letter to the city. Eleven is home to Claire, Glenn, John, Alys, Josie and Kathryn; five natives and one Welshman who now happily calls Sheffield his home. Every place in this book is handpicked by us.

elevendesign.co.uk

EAT

Our food section is split into an easy-to-digest series of Top 3s. Many restaurants and cafes would easily slot into multiple categories, but these mini lists should give you a good place to start. And, when it comes to eating in Sheffield, don't be put off by first impressions of a place: we've found that some of the best food in the city is served in some of the most unassuming surroundings. Dig in!

BREAKFAST

◆ Tamper

Sheffield will be forever in debt to Tamper for introducing it to the joys of hearty, New Zealand-inspired breakfasts and brunches.

Eggs crop up all over the menu, cooked to your liking. And while beans on toast may not sound like much of a treat, Tamper's take on the classic is something else entirely.

Breakfast is served until midday, but if you're a little late out of bed, we'd recommend the sweetcorn and chilli fritters, topped off with poached eggs. Also keep an eye out for Tamper Lates, when the cafe opens into the evening with a changing (always delicious) menu.

See p19 for more on Tamper.

Tamper Sellers Wheel,
149 Arundel Street, S1 2NU
0114 275 7970
tampercoffee.co.uk

Tamper, by Shaun Bloodworth

Okeh Cafe, by Shaun Bloodworth, courtesy of the University of Sheffield

◆ Okeh Cafe

Meeting place for scooter clubs and Mod throwbacks. As the jukebox spins its rhythm and blues, slide into a leatherette booth, tuck into a classic greasy spoon breakfast (served all day and ridiculously cheap) with a mug of coffee, and let yourself be transported back to the sixties.

116 Abbeydale Road, S7 1FF

◆ Ceres

An easygoing French place right on Hunter's Bar, Ceres is brilliant for breakfast – their creamy pan-fried mushrooms have set us up for many walks to nearby Forge Dam. Check out their bistro nights too, starting around 5pm Wed-Sat the pleasingly simple menu is deservedly popular – so book ahead!

85 Junction Road, S11 8XA
0114 267 9090
cafeceres.com

The Greedy Greek, by Glenn at Eleven

◆ Street Food Chef

Nachos, churros and luminous Jarritos…
we love the Street Food Chef! Any excuse
and we're there, whether it's for an
afternoon quesadilla between shops, or a
pre-cinema pan fried burrito. Head to the
Chef's hole-in-the-wall on Pinstone Street
for a quick takeaway, or its cantina on
Arundel Street for a sit-down meal.
Beware the Mexican Hot salsa: it brought
tears to our eyes – and we're pretty hard,
you know.

Open every day. The takeaway closes at
5pm (4pm on a Sunday) but the cantina
stays open until 10pm.

Eat in: 90 Arundel Street, S1 4RE
0114 275 2390
Takeaway: 98 Pinstone Street, S1 2HQ
0114 273 7909
streetfoodchef.co.uk

◆ Greedy Greek

When the sun shines over Hunters Bar, nothing can beat picking up a bulging falafel and halloumi wrap from the Greedy Greek, taking it over the road to Endcliffe Park, and wrestling it into your mouth before the cherry tomatoes make a run for it and the hummus oozes out over your fingers. For a real Greek feast – full of olives, dips, spanakopita, and herby chips – pick up a bottle of wine on the way and eat in.

420 Sharrow Vale Road, S11 8ZP
0114 266 7719
thegreedygreekdeli.co.uk

◆ Fry Masters

Nestled amongst the slightly odd shops of Attercliffe (think snakes, model cars and sex toys) is Fry Masters, aka fish & chip heaven. Park yourself in a booth and take your pick of the fishy meals on offer; you'll get a handsome piece of cod, haddock or plaice, with chips, and peas, beans or gravy, plus lavishly buttered bread and a cup of tea – all this, AND change from a fiver.

653 Attercliffe Road, S9 3RE
0114 327 2303

The Street Food Chef, by Shaun Bloodworth

◆ VeroGusto

Settle down with an aperitif in this pretty pale blue restaurant and make sure you have a good appetite. You'll want one for VeroGusto's gourmet Italian antipasti, secondi and dessert (leave room – they're fantastico!). So authentic, you could be in a bustling Napoli restaurant (where the owners are from). Top marks for food, wine, service and atmosphere.

Open Tue-Sat 4-10pm

12 Norfolk Row, S1 2PA
0114 276 0004
gustosheffield.co.uk

◆ Greenhead House

A quaint place to the north of the city, Greenhead House is a 17th century cottage, offering four-course meals, plus canapés and petit fours, in its small dining room. When the sun's out, enjoy aperitifs and coffee in the lovely walled garden.

84 Burncross Road,
Chapeltown, S35 1SF
0114 246 9004
greenheadhouse.com

◆ Rafters

Creative cooking and a cracking wine list set this cosy restaurant apart. Not far from Endcliffe Park, Rafters is full of in-the-know Sheffield foodies tucking into spiced/smoked/roasted delicacies, washed down with expertly matched wines.

220 Oakbrook Road,
Nether Green, S11 7ED
0114 230 4819
raftersrestaurant.co.uk

Illustrations by Glenn at Eleven

◆ Rutland Arms

The Rutland's halloumi burger is the best thing to have ever touched crockery in Sheffield. It brings a smile to our face and a warmth to our tummy just thinking about it. They do meaty burgers too, and the bhaji butty is great – but we're all about the halloumi.

86 Brown Street, S1 2BS
0114 272 9003
rutlandarmspeople.co.uk

If you find yourself up Crookesmoor way, the Rutland's sibling pub The Closed Shop (p25) has a similar menu (including the revered halloumi burger).

52-54 Commonside, S10 1GG
0114 266 0330
theclosedshopsheffield.co.uk

◆ Twisted Burger Co. at The Harley

Sticky structures oozing sauce, cheese and excess. The pun-heavy menu includes In Da Club, This Is Hardcore and Falaf-hell – which offers some indication of the levels of decadence you're dealing with here. Fries come topped with all manner of sauce/spice/garnish combos. Nothing in moderation.

334 Glossop Road, S10 2HW
0114 275 2288
theharley.co.uk

◆ Homemade by Thelma's – Burger Nights

Wednesday night is burger and shake night at this super Nether Edge cafe and bistro. Served with proper chips, a side of premium coleslaw, and plated up the American way (i.e. in a basket), the burgers are divine. Loads of choice for vegetarian, vegan and gluten-free folk too.

Burger nights are currently a spring-summer event, but fingers crossed they'll make it year-round! Call ahead to book. Friday bistro nights are also well worth a visit, and the daytime salads are fab.

4 Nether Edge Road, S7 1RU
homemade-sheffield.co.uk

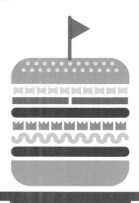

◆ Jameson's

Sparkly chandeliers, linen tablecloths and a fabulous spread of sticky buns, enormous scones and lovely homemade cakes makes this traditional and gorgeous family-run tea room our go-to place when we're craving something sweet. Which is often.

334 Abbeydale Road, S7 1FN
0114 255 1159
jamesonstearooms.co.uk

Electric Candlelight Cafe, by Shaun Bloodworth

◆ Electric Candlelight Cafe

Named after a line from 'Lola' by the Kinks, the Electric Candlelight Cafe is run by long-time member of Sheffield's musical family tree, Paul Infanti. Always fabulously turned out in cowboy boots and a ten-gallon hat, Paul dishes out decadent and delicious cakes in this gorgeous corner cafe... not something you see too often.

With furnishings from neighbour Vintedge, it's such a treat to spend some time in Paul's world, with Candlelight's own coffee blend and a gold glittery brownie.

Brunch is ace too – we like to settle down at the quiet chess table by the window with the papers and something eggy.

448 Abbeydale Road, S7 1FR

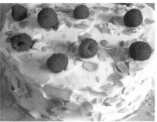

Image courtesy of Harland Cafe

◆ Harland Cafe

A calming retreat set back from the bustle of London Road. Fab breakfasts, lovely owners, and always something exciting happening. Poetry evenings, family activities, couscous suppers... but what really keeps us coming back are the huge homemade cakes. Delicious!

72 John Street, S2 4QU
0114 273 8553
harlandcafe.co.uk

The Mediterranean, by Nigel Barker

◆ The Mediterranean

Our absolute favourite restaurant, the Mediterranean is a gem. Top notch, fantastically fresh food served by super friendly staff. The atmosphere is relaxed and the manager, Otto, a superb host. If we had to choose our last meal, it would be a seafood feast from here.

271 Sharrow Vale Road, S11 8ZF
0114 266 1069
mediterraneansheffield.co.uk

◆ Patoo

After a busy week, nothing beats a Friday night feast in Patoo. We always order the same thing: gung ma noa (prawns steamed with ginger, lemon, chilli and garlic) and pla choo-chee (deep-fried fish in red curry sauce) and, of course, a round of Singha beers. If you try anything else then please let us know what it's like!

607 Ecclesall Road, S11 8PT
0114 266 8196
patoothai.com

◆ Two Steps

The best fish & chips in Sheffield. By far. The Friday teatime queue is testament to the perfection of Two Steps, whose reputation dates back to 1895. Mmmm, dandelion and burdock too.

249 Sharrow Vale Road, S11 8ZE
0114 266 5694
twostepssheffield.co.uk

Two Steps, by Claire at Eleven

◆ Fanoush

Back in spring 2011, we got super excited when we peeked through a newspapered window on London Road to see 'falafel' written in tile on the back wall. When Fanoush opened, its packed flatbread wraps, salad boxes and multiple hummus flavours did not disappoint. Falafel Friday quickly became a tradition for us; now, with three branches across the city, every day can be a falafel day! Add aubergine/cauliflower/halloumi/feta for an extra treat.

103 London Road, S2 4LE
100 Pinstone Street, S1 2HQ
208 Whitham Road, S10 2SS

◆ Elif

A fresh kebab from Elif cannot be beaten for a tea-time takeaway. We go so often they know our order as soon as they see us: one veggie kebab and one chicken – with chilli sauce, of course.

Open every evening from 5pm.

529 Ecclesall Road, S11 8PR
0114 266 6876

◆ QC's Bagel Bar

So much fun to be had checking off Sheffield landmarks against their namesake on QC's menu: from the River Sheaf to Hallam, via the Winter Garden and Ponds Forge – many of the city's distinct features have bagels named after them. Who knew Devonshire Green could be so tasty?

Open midweek til 2:30pm.

8 Orchard Street, S1 2GX
0114 272 1985

Illustrations by Glenn at Eleven

◆ The Broadfield

Pies and sausages: it doesn't get more comforting than this. The Broadfield's menu features daily specials of each, including decent vegetarian options. They're not short on options for washing down their delicious meals either, with a bar lined with ales and whiskies from near and far. After your meal move across into the busy bar area and snap up a booth, beautifully put together from reclaimed railway doors during the pub's restoration in 2011. Food served every day 11:30am-10pm

452 Abbeydale Road, S7 1FR
0114 255 0200
thebroadfield.co.uk

◆ Endcliffe Park Cafe

All we ever have from this cafe is egg & chips (sometimes beans), but it's always packed – so the rest of the substantial menu must be equally as good. For us though, it's all about the runniness of the egg and the fluffiness of the chip. Best to go when it's warm(ish) so you can sit outside and enjoy your fry-up with a blast of fresh air. From here, walk through the park to Forge Dam where you'll find another great cafe selling local ice creams for the walk back.

Endcliffe Park, Rustlings Road,
S11 7AB
0114 266 3044
endcliffeparkcafe.com

Endcliffe Park Cafe, by Claire at Eleven

◆ Bloo 88

Dough and melted cheese – that's our idea of comfort. Fresh from the stone bake oven, Bloo's pizzas are the tastiest in town. It can get busy with the cocktail crowd later on, so best to head there in the afternoon or early evening.

182 West Street, S1 4ET
0114 270 6264
bloo88.com

The Broadfield, by Shaun Bloodworth

CURRY

◆ Zara's

Best pickle tray in Sheffield, and some of the tastiest, freshest curries. If you've room for a pint afterwards, you'll find The Closed Shop (p25) and Hallamshire House (p22) ten minutes away on Commonside.

216 Crookes, S10 1TH
0114 266 0097
zarasrestaurant.com

◆ 7 Spices

After being drawn in by the bright neon sign, you descend into a subterranean kingdom of curry. The décor's a little odd, with its Greco Roman arches and Hawaiian themed bar, but don't worry about that – get yourself a cold Tiger beer and try not to over-order.

129 Mayfair Court, West Bar, S3 8PP
0114 275 7695
7spicesbalti.co.uk

◆ Indo Lanka Fusion
(formerly East & West)

Blink and you'll miss this tiny South Indian and Sri Lankan canteen and takeaway amidst the antique shops and pretty cafes of Abbeydale Road. Despite its size, it dishes up some of the tastiest, cheapest and spiciest food in Sheffield, from chilli paneer to masala dosa (a huge pancake with curry in the middle = one of the world's greatest culinary inventions). They have a bigger place in Crookes too: Rama's Bridge.

227 Abbeydale Road, S7 1FJ
0114 258 8066
eastnwest.net

7 Spices, by Glenn at Eleven

The Rude Shipyard, by Shaun Bloodworth

VEGGIE
CHOICE

◆ The Rude Shipyard

Super cute cafe-cum-bookshop, the Rude Shipyard offers an ever-changing selection of tasty vegan and vegetarian lunches, as well as ace Guinness cake and a shelf full of tea options. Open 10am-4pm every day except Wed. Also, keep an eye out for their Thursday Suppers for an evening tastebud-treat.

89 Abbeydale Road, S7 1FE
0114 258 9653
therudeshipyard.com

◆ Little Hanoi

Vietnamese food with plenty of choice for veggies and vegans, including proper tofu – crispy on the outside and custardy in the middle. Our favourite thing about Little Hanoi is that the veggie stuff is actually properly labelled – there's no ambiguity about fish sauce here. There's also a Karaoke room upstairs. YES! KARAOKE!

216 London Road, S2 4LW
0114 258 3836

◆ Blue Moon

Wholesome food, organic wine and plentiful salads in a lovely setting, this fantastic vegan and vegetarian cafe is housed in a former auction house, next door to the cathedral. Always busy, try and arrive before the lunchtime rush or you may have a bit of a wait. Don't forget to look up – the ceiling is beautiful.

2 St James Row, S1 2EW
0114 276 3443

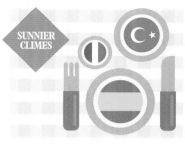

SUNNIER CLIMES

◆ Lokanta

Lokanta's hearty Turkish dishes are served with some of the best dips we've ever tasted, and there's loads of meat-free choices included on their long list of meze dishes, kebabs and Anatolian-inspired specials. End with Yee Kwan's amazing Turkish Delight ice-cream.

478 Glossop Road, Broomhill, S10 2QA
0114 266 6444
lokanta.co.uk

◆ La Terrazza

Cosy, friendly and authentic. The kind of Italian restaurant everyone wishes was their local – we're very fortunate that La Terrazza is ours! Cappellini di zucca is our dish of choice, washed down with a glass or two of their artisan red wine. Delish.

352 Sharrow Vale Road, S11 8ZP
0114 268 5150
laterrazza.co.uk

◆ El Toro

El Toro brings authentic dishes from Madrid to this tiny canteen and tapas bar in Broomhill. With a menu that changes daily to utilise the freshest seasonal market produce. It's just down the road from The York should you fancy a pre/post tapas tipple (p24).

129 Newbould Lane,
Broomhill, S10 2PL
0114 2666956
el-toro-sheffield.co.uk

Blue Moon, by Shaun Bloodworth, courtesy of the University of Sheffield

FOOD MILE

Running just south of the city centre for about a mile, London Road and the start of Abbeydale Road pack more choice when it comes to eating out than almost anywhere else in Sheffield.

Sushi, kebabs, oodles of noodles, curries, burritos, tapas, teppenyaki, meze – there's so much on offer here we couldn't possibly fit it all into our little book.

Below are just a few of our favourites – pick up our World Food Tour for more; ourfaveplaces.bigcartel.com

◆ La Mama

We get that the point of tapas is to share, but this lovely Latin restaurant makes it really difficult – everything on the menu tastes so great that we just want it all to ourselves!

238 Abbeydale Road, S7 1FL
0114 327 9597
lamama-sheffield.blogspot.co.uk

◆ Amici & Bici

A cafe fit for cycling fanatics – there's space to park bikes outside and Lycra is the accepted attire inside. The Tour de France and other big bike races are screened on TV, which you can watch as you drink from cups printed with cute bicycle motifs. Cycling memorabilia dots the walls and pretty racing bikes frame the view through the windows. Great cakes, too.

220 Abbeydale Road, S7 1FL
0114 438 2776

◆ Zeugma

Head to this atmospheric place for the most authentic Turkish fare, served fresh from the open grill. Everyone we know who's eaten here has loved it, and each generally has a favourite dish. Try to book, as it's always busy – so much so that they opened a second restaurant, Zeugma Iki, a bit further along the road.

146 London Road, S2 4LT
0114 258 2223
zeugmaiki.com

◆ Dim Sum

Please check out the incredibly endearing website for Dim Sum: www.dimsum-sheffield.co.uk...

"Shall we go 'Yum Cha' and have some 'Dim Sum'?"

And then please give it a try. We've tasted most of the steamed dim sum snacks here (never braved the whelks though), and we love it.

201 London Road, S2 4LJ
0114 255 0467
dimsum-sheffield.co.uk

See also:

Illustrations by Glenn at Eleven

DRINK

Cafes, pubs, bars – there's no shortage of watering holes to choose from in Sheffield. That's why we've organised our favourites according to what we reckon they do best – from the best coffee, to the best places to sit with a paper, to the pub with the greatest view. We hope you're thirsty!

COFFEE

◆ Bragazzi's

There's nowhere nicer to recuperate from an afternoon spent pottering around the Antiques Quarter (p48) than this fantastico Italian cafe (below). The delicious aroma of espresso and panini is impossible to ignore and, as well summer gelato and their own distinct coffee blend, there's the added bonus of its decor – the best in Sheffield.

220 Abbeydale Road, S7 1FL
0114 258 1483
bragazzis.co.uk

Bragazzi's, by Shaun Bloodworth

◆ Steam Yard

Set back in the cobbled courtyard of what was a 19th century silver and electro-plate works, Steam Yard's leather booths and low-hanging lampshades offer a cosy hideaway. Like Sheffield's best coffee shops, Steam Yard's house blend is roasted locally at Pollards. It also serves the biggest doughnuts in the city.

Aberdeen Court,
95-101 Division Street, S1 4GN

◆ Remo's

Until they moved up the road to a larger spot, it was often impossible to squeeze in to this Italian cafe, particularly around lunch time. Seek it out and allow yourself to be tempted by their dessert menu – you won't be disappointed.

259 Fulwood Road, Broomhill,
S10 3BD

◆ Motoré

As you may infer from its name, Motoré serves coffees from the back of a motor vehicle – a beautifully-restored Piaggo Ape, to be precise. The Motoré van can be found parked up on Howard Street in all weathers (7:30am-2:30pm Mon-Fri) and, conveniently, is right on the pathway leading out from Sheffield station. Pick up a tasty biscotti or a Sicilian pastry with your artisan coffee-to-go, and walk uphill to the city centre in real Italian style.

Howard Street, S1 2LW

◆ Tamper

The small but perfectly-formed Tamper on Westfield Terrace is full of charm and the heady smells of freshly-roasted gourmet coffee. The owner, Jonathan, is an expert barista from New Zealand who, lucky for us, brought his passion and knowledge for the bean to our hilly city. Great food too (award-winning pies, top flapjacks) and super-friendly service.

Tamper Sellers Wheel opened to quench Sheffield's thirst for their unbeatable flat whites and long blacks. The new site (below) has the same look as the original – reclaimed furniture, exposed brickwork – but is much bigger, with an extensive food menu and great beer from of The Hop Box.

9 Westfield Terrace, S1 4GH
0114 327 1080

Sellers Wheel,
149 Arundel Street, S1 2NU
0114 275 7970

tampercoffee.co.uk

See also: Top 3 for Breakfast, p2

Tamper, by Shaun Bloodworth

◆ The Old House

After guzzling our way across the city, we can say with conviction that Sheffield's best cocktails are shaken, or stirred, at the Old House. Knowledgeable bar staff are keen to ensure that you find a drink that hits the spot, be it fruity, sour, sharp or sweet. You'll find all the classics, plus some that are adapted to give them a new twist, but it's the in-house creations you should take a sip of.

113 Devonshire Street, S3 7SB
0114 276 6002
theoldhousesheffield.com

◆ The Great Gatsby

A Flamingo cocktail in the 'beard garden' out back (with its loveable beardy character mural painted by Sheffield's own Nick Deakin) is bliss on a summer's evening. Great DJs 'til late on weekends, the occasional gig upstairs, and top food courtesy of Shy Boy Cantina make this an all-round smashing city-centre bar.

73 Division Street, S1 4GE
0114 273 1050
thegatsbybar.co.uk

◆ The Washington

Music is the beating heart of the Washy. Band posters of Sheffield favourites – Pulp, ABC, Richard Hawley – and '80s album sleeve corkers line the walls, crowds regularly squeeze in to see the latest local acts, and an eclectic roster of DJs take turns at the decks. On Friday and Saturday nights the sizeable beer garden is as lively and fun as the dance floor.

79 Fitzwilliam Street, S1 4JP
0114 276 1960
washingtonsheffield.com

◆ The Lescar

A brilliant pub with a local feel and laid-back in the best possible way – the Lescar is hard to beat. Go for live jazz on a Wednesday night and guaranteed good tunes at the weekend.

303 Sharrow Vale Road, S11 8ZF
0114 266 8974
jazzatthelescar.com

We also have to mention the superb jukebox at the Porter Cottage (p25). PJ Harvey always seems to come on when we're in there, and we like it that way.

See also: Music, p36

◆ Cafe No. 9

Cafe No. 9 is like nowhere else in the city, and is our idea of cafe perfection. Somehow it managed to evade our attention for years, but we're making up for lost time now: we can't get enough of the place, with it's wood lined interior, chess sets, ace music and warm cinnamon rolls. Take your pick from their piles of papers and escape from the world on the other side of the window for an hour or two. **TOP TIP:** don't miss the mobile pizza oven on a Wednesday tea time.

9 Nether Edge Road, S7 1RU
0114 258 1383

◆ Green City Coffee

A tranquil place tucked a little bit away from the city centre in Kelham Island, close to the museum (p57). Sink into a settee with a crossword, or one of the books or games from the shelf, and while away your afternoon. Literary readings and music events are often held on evenings and weekends.

1 Kelham Island Square, S3 8SD
0114 272 1346
greencitycoffee.co.uk

◆ The Old Horns Inn

Take your drink out to a picnic
table, sit down, and breathe in
the calming, fresh air of the Peaks
as you gaze out across the rolling
Bradfield Moors. Beautiful.

High Bradfield, S6 6LG
0114 285 1207
theoldhorns.co.uk

The Old Horns Inn, by Nigel Barker

◆ The Hallamshire House

Done up in recent years, there's
several reasons the Hallamshire is
worth a special trip out of town:
great ales (many brewed by the
pub's owners Thornbridge, inc.
the dreamy Chiron), a beautiful
snooker room (it's now the only
pub in Sheffield to have a full-size
snooker table), and its proximity
to the charity shop delights of
Crookes. Partially under cover, its
beer garden can be enjoyed
come rain or shine!

49-51 Commonside, S10 1GF
0114 266 4466
myhallamshire.co.uk

◆ Rutland Arms

Take a seat in the beer garden and enjoy a pint and an infamous Rutty Butty amongst the hydrangeas. We've raved enough about the Rutland's food (p7), but we also love the place for its tiled facade, its position smack-bang in city's busiest cultural spot (close to Site Gallery, Yorkshire Artspace, the Showroom, Bloc and Mary Street), and its staff's enthusiasm for real ale.

86 Brown Street, S1 2BS
0114 272 9003
rutlandarmspeople.co.uk

◆ The Forum

The blue and white tiling in the Forum's outdoor seating area always makes us feel a little like we're by a swimming pool… but that's cool! The Forum is popular for eating and drinking, and is loads of fun. In summer, pick up an orange deckchair and laze away the afternoon people-spotting across Devonshire Green.

127-129 Devonshire Street, S3 7SB
0114 272 0569
forumsheffield.co.uk

See also:
The Broadfield, p12
The Riverside, p27
The Fat Cat, p26

Sheffield Tap, by Nigel Barker

◆ Sheffield Tap

Originally a 'refreshment room' for first class rail passengers, what is now the Tap stood empty and in disrepair for thirty years. Two locals sniffed it out and restored it to its original splendour, complete with Edwardian tiles and salvaged mahogany bar. Selling 200+ beers from around the world – with 22 on draught – and brewing their own in vats in the back room, the Tap feels European and local at the same time.

Platform 1b, Sheffield Station,
Sheaf Street, S1 2BP
0114 273 7558
sheffieldtap.com

◆ The York

In the days of toll roads, The York was a stop-off point for travellers between Sheffield and Glossop. Back when it first opened (in the 1830s), it doubled up as ale house and blacksmiths. Today, the pub's cosy interior – with glazed tiles and rich, dark colours – is a celebration of its Victorian heritage. As well as the atmosphere, enjoy the homemade chutneys, smoked cheeses (straight from the on-site smokehouse) and cocktails. Just watch your shins on the anvil.

243-247 Fulwood Road,
Broomhill, S10 3BA
0114 266 4624
theyorksheffield.co.uk

◆ The Closed Shop

Try and spot the theme early on: once you've got Tiger Woods, Snakes on a Plane and Cat Stevens on your answer sheet, a pattern is clearly forming, and – if nothing else – it makes any guesswork a little less misguided. Sundays, from 8pm.

52-54 Commonside, S10 1GG
0114 266 0330
theclosedshopsheffield.co.uk

◆ Porter Cottage

Taking a different, fairly loose, theme each week – categories include 'us and the world', music, art, books and film. At the midway point something really special happens: grown-ups grapple like school kids for straws, sheets of foil and elastic bands to build elaborate sculptures for the art round. Tuesdays, from 9pm.

286 Sharrow Vale Road, S11 8ZL
0114 268 7412

◆ The Blake

A pleasingly simple quiz – 20 questions, no messing around. The Blake is a handsome pub; all Victorian fixtures and etched windows, and the beer and whisky selection is tip top, so plenty to distract you if you do badly in the quiz. Sitting upon Sheffield's steepest hill, you'll be rewarded with cracking views of the city as you stumble home. Wednesdays from 9pm.

53 Blake Street, S6 3JQ
0114 233 9336

See also: The Riverside, p27

◆ The Bath Hotel

At the corner of a row of mid-Victorian terraces, this pub has changed very little since the early 20th century. Its historical significance is marked out by the blue Tetley Heritage Inn plaque by the door. A perfect pub: relaxed, welcoming, beautiful tiled floors and stained-glass windows, and a great atmosphere – think groups of locals cosying up to the fire and solving crosswords over a Sheffield-brewed beer.

66-68 Victoria Street, S3 7QL
0114 249 5151
beerinthebath.co.uk

◆ Kelham Island Tavern

Originally opened in the 1830s, the Kelham Island Tavern has become the jewel in the Real Ale quarter, winning CAMRA's National Pub of The Year in 2007 and 2008. During the summer months, the Tavern is ideal for outdoor drinking, with its exotic palm tree-lined beer garden acting as a beacon for folk music, morris dancers and real ale enthusiasts.

62 Russell Street, S3 8RW
0114 272 2482
kelhamtavern.co.uk

◆ The Fat Cat

The Fat Cat was the first boozer to break free of the Big Breweries — becoming a real ale free house in 1981. An open policy on its taps has seen the Fat Cat pull nearly 8000 different beers in the past 30 years — including its own beer garden-based brewery. A great place to grab an adventurous ale and a hot pork pie.

23 Alma Street, S3 8SA
0114 249 4801
thefatcat.co.uk

◆ The Ship Inn

The Ship Inn is a slice of sea-faring life in the heart of the former industrial quarter, with maritime paraphernalia adorning the pub's three spaces. Spookily, the ghosts of two sailors that drowned in secret tunnels under the pub during the 1864 Sheffield floods are said to frequently pop in for the odd jar of local ale.

312 Shalesmoor, S3 8UL
0114 221 1689

Illustration by John at Eleven

◆ The Wellington

The Wellington, just off Shalesmoor tram stop, has a humble exterior that belies its cosy rooms. This four-time Sheffield Pub of the Year is a classic, traditional snug full of warmth and personality serving well conditioned cask ales. Pale, hoppy beers made by the on-site Little Ale Cart brewery dominate the hand-pumps, whilst also featuring a wide selection of bottled Belgian classics.

1 Henry Street, S3 7EQ
0114 249 2295

◆ The Riverside

Sitting alongside the River Don, The Riverside exists in its own little world. The bar features refreshing continental and American keg beers, crisp pilsners and hoppy IPAs – perfect for refreshing the palate after all that Kelham Island Real Ale.

Its large beer garden, heated riverside terrace, frequent barbeques and gigs make the Riverside a must visit destination in the summer months.

Quiz nights (Mondays, from 8pm) are also superb, with a good mix of trivia and brainteasers and extra points dished out on whims. Eight pints for the winning team!

1 Mowbray Street, S3 8EN
0114 272 4640
riversidesheffield.co.uk

◆

If you want more Real Ale tips – and who doesn't – look out for our Real Ale Trail;
ourfaveplaces.bigcartel.com

Words by Greg Povey

Graves Gallery, by Nigel Barker

◆ Graves Gallery

Above Sheffield's Central Library, the Graves feels like a bit of a secret. Opened in 1934, the collections span the 16th-21st centuries and include Cézanne, Turner, Bridget Riley, Patrick Caulfield, and Sam Taylor-Wood. When you reach the top floor, by stairs or the rickety lift, look down the stairwell over the beautiful cascade of blue and purple pieces of yarn (woven by Sheffield-based artist Seiko Kinoshita), before losing yourself in the work and the splendour of your 1930s surroundings.

Open Wed-Fri 10am-3pm, Sat 11am-4pm

Surrey Street, S1 1XZ
0114 278 2600
museums-sheffield.org.uk

◆ Millennium Gallery

Even if we only plan on cutting through to get to the Winter Gardens, something at the Millennium Gallery inevitably catches our eye and makes us stick around – whether it's a glinting through the window of the Metalwork Collection, a peek at the beautifully illustrated books in the Ruskin Collection, or a new addition to the gift shop. It has a great programme of large-scale temporary exhibitions to boot.

Open Mon-Sat 10am-5pm, Sun 11am-4pm

Arundel Gate, S1 2PP
0114 278 2600
museums-sheffield.org.uk

◆ Site Gallery

Sheffield's dedicated contemporary art space, Site has an exciting international programme showing renowned and emerging artists, who have often never before exhibited in the UK. Just down the road from the Showroom Cinema and a two-minute walk from the Millennium and Graves galleries, Site should be on the must-see list of every art fan. Also houses a super cafe and a shop packed with amazing art books, independent magazines and smashing gifts.

Open Tue-Sat 11am-5:30pm

1 Brown Street, S1 2BS
0114 281 2077
sitegalley.org

Site Gallery, by Peter Martin

◆ S1 Artspace

Founded by a group of Sheffield-based artists in 1995, S1 Artspace is a cultural treat of exhibitions, screenings and events.

Somewhat tucked away, though only a 10-minute walk from Site or Bloc, seek out S1 for one of the best contemporary art programmes in Sheffield, as well as some of the best parties.

Open Wed-Sat 12-6pm

120 Trafalgar Street, S1 4JT
0114 213 3780
s1artspace.org

◆ Bloc Projects

This teeny-tiny project space delivers an eclectic programme. Check the site for the exhibition launch nights – they draw a good crowd for pre-show beers in the courtyard.

Open Wed-Sat 12-6pm

71 Eyre Lane, S1 4RB
0114 272 3155
blocprojects.co.uk

◆ APG Works

In the middle of the art triangle formed by Site, Mary Street and Bloc, pop into APG while you're in the area. A printing and framing studio as well as a gallery, most of the exhibitions in this former cutlery factory feature contemporary printmakers.

Open Mon-Sat 11am-4pm

16-20 Sidney Street, S1 4RH
0114 263 4493
apgworks.co.uk

◆ Bank Street Arts

From poetry and music events in its airy atrium, to contemporary art and photography exhibitions in its galleries, it's always worth taking a look at what's on in this arts centre. The biennial Sheffield International Artist's Book Prize exhibition is not to be missed.

Open Wed-Sat 11am-4pm

32-40 Bank Street, S1 2DS
0114 346 3034
bankstreetarts.com

S1 Artspace: Eva Berendes, *People and Events will be the Decoration* [installation view]

99 Mary Street, by Nynke Wierda Photography

◆ 99 Mary Street

Mary Street's cobbles have become well frequented by devotees of contemporary art and design since the doors to no. 99 opened and their neighbours Bradbury and Blanchard moved in. Owned by design studio DED, 99MS has got off to a promising start with some curious exhibitions and cracking launch parties.

Open Mon-Fri 10:30am-5pm during exhibitions, and Saturday by appointment.

99 Mary Street, S1 4RT
0114 273 1799
99mary.st

◆ B&B Gallery

The eponymous B&B are Ed Bradbury and Florence Blanchard, a pair of artists turned curators who set up this gallery and screen-printing studio in 2013. Their fab programme encompasses artists both emerging and established, local and international. Slightly off-centre, plan your visit to also take in the gallery at 99 Mary Street, and hit the cobbles!

Open Sat 12-6pm during exhibitions – at other times by appointment.

95b Mary Street, S1 4RT
bandbgallery.com

FILM

◆ Showroom

Converted from a 1930s Art Deco car showroom, this four-screen independent cinema is one of the places we hold dearest in Sheffield. Alongside the latest art-house films and indie docs, the Showroom regularly dusts off rarely-screened reels for its educational programmes and Cult Tuesday screenings. Kids are kept busy with crafts and films at Saturday Club, while pensioners are treated to coffee and cake at Early Doors on Thursday mornings. Festivals here include the superb Doc/Fest (held in June), Celluloid Screams, Sheffield Adventure Film Festival, and, for the kids, Showcomotion.

Great bar, too, with a monthly quiz for real film buffs and regular free screenings of short, largely locally-made films. We were pleased as punch to have our own film projected here once – you can find it on our Vimeo channel: vimeo.com/ourfaveplaces.

15 Paternoster Row, S1 2BX
0114 275 7727
showroomworkstation.org.uk

◆

The Showroom illustration is by We Live Here, the instantly-recognisable work of Sheffield-based artist Jonathan Wilkinson. We love We Live Here's pared-down graphic representations of our city and are chuffed to have one in our book. Thanks Jonathan!

welivehere.co.uk

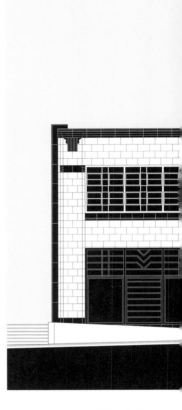

◆ Magic Lantern Film Club

An intermittent programme of cult and classic cinematic treats projected in a different space each time – from an old school hall to a bike yard, a cosy pub to an echoing warehouse. Magic Lantern does a smashing job of bringing communities together for intimate and unforgettable encounters with moving pictures.

magiclanternfilmclub.wordpress.com

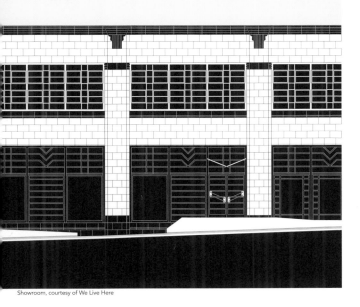

Showroom, courtesy of We Live Here

◆ Film Unit

Run by student volunteers for over sixty years, Film Unit turns Sheffield Students' Union auditorium into a cinema each term-time weekend. Friday nights tend to offer something a little cultish, while other screenings include documentaries and independent films a few months on from their general release. And the best part? Tickets cost £2.50. Yes, £2.50.

Sheffield Students' Union,
Western Bank, S10 2TG
filmunit.org.uk

◆ Sharrow Reels

Coffee, cake and a film – the perfect way to end a weekend. Sharrow Reels put on a film one Sunday evening a month in an old chapel. Just £3 all in.

Crowded House,
215 Sharrow Vale Road, S11 8ZB
sharrowreels.wordpress.com

◆ THEATRE

◆ Crucible Theatre

Sheffield's iconic and beloved theatre has been on top form since its grand reopening. An impressive line-up have trodden the boards of this unusual-shaped theatre. The thrust stage means the audience sits on three sides and no one is more than 22 metes away from the performance – ensuring an atmospheric and intimate experience.

The Crucible, its Studio theatre and its sister the Lyceum, form the country's largest theatre complex outside of London. Shows span drama, dance, comedy and, of course, snooker (the World Snooker Championships are held here) – so you should find something to suit.

55 Norfolk Street, S1 1DA
0114 249 6000
sheffieldtheatres.co.uk

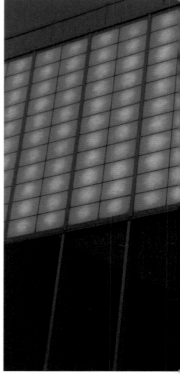

Illustration by John at Eleven

Crucible Theatre, by Shaun Bloodworth, courtesy of the University of Sheffield

◆ Lantern Theatre

The Lantern is incredible. Built as a private theatre in 1886 by wealthy cutler William Webster, for use by his family, it was left derelict after WW2. It was restored to its former glory in the 1950s by Dilys Guite, a local actor and drama teacher.

This tiny Victorian theatre still hosts the Dilys Guite Players as well as other amateur groups, comedy nights, and all kinds of music. The venue itself is so charming we would urge you to go and see whatever is on.

Kenwood Park Road, S7 1NF
0114 255 1776
lanternthetre.org.uk

◆ Library Theatre

Tucked behind Sheffield's beautiful Central Library, and in the same square as the Crucible and the Lyceum, is the atmospheric Library Theatre.

This art deco theatre feels like a bit of a secret – for years we didn't even know it existed! Its programme is a mix of am-dram, comedy, local history and music, and the under-the-radar vibe only adds to the enjoyment. During the war it was used as an air raid shelter and for showing Ministry of Information films – it's your civic duty to visit!

Surrey Street, S1 1XZ
0114 273 4712
sheffield.gov.uk/libraries/librarytheatre

Image courtesy of The Harley

MUSIC

Greystones

On no other stage have we seen as wide, wonderful and – in certain cases – weird a range of acoustic instruments. The Greystones' listings often throw up pleasant surprises, and the dimly lit back room is full of speakeasy character. And, we love that David Lynch watches over proceedings from his black-and-white portrait on the wall.

Greystones Road, S11 7BS
0114 266 5599
mygreystones.co.uk

Sheffield Jazz

For two packed seasons each year, Sheffield Jazz perks up the city and gets toes tapping with their incredible international line-up of musicians.

Most events held at Millennium Hall, 518 Ecclesall Road, S11 8PY
sheffieldjazz.org.uk

The Harley

If you paid attention to our tip-off (p7) you may already have tucked into a burger at the Harley. Its gigs should keep you sticking around too. Listings include the sorts of new bands that are starting to creep onto the Radio 6 playlist, as well as favourites of any genre from indie-pop to hip hop via garage-blues-rock. And if you're up for a dance, its club nights will keep you entertained 'til late. We've had some fun at the Harley in our time.

Also look out for gigs put on by the Harley beneath the stone arches of Sheffield Cathedral or on the charming tinsel-draped stage of the Queens Social Club.

334 Glossop Road, S10 2HW
0114 275 2288
harleylive.co.uk

◆ The Audacious Art Experiment

Set up and managed the DIY way, this record label has pressed to vinyl/cassette/CD some of the most original and exciting bands to come from Sheffield and beyond in recent years. These good-natured folk frequently make way in their practice space for gigs, too: often loud, sometimes rowdy, always fun.

Harwood Street, S2 4SE
theaudaciousartexperiment.com

◆ Heeley Institute

In what was a Victorian chapel, this community centre now puts on the occasional intimate gig towards the folkier end of the acoustic spectrum.

147 Gleadless Road, S2 3AE
0114 250 0613

◆ The University of Sheffield Concerts

We're no experts when it comes to classical, jazz or world music, so we're pretty thankful to Uni Concerts for helping make each that bit more accessible. The programme includes lunchtime, rush-hour and evening shows, plus talks, and special seasons focussing on innovators from the history of music. An extra perk: most performances take place within the magnificent Firth Hall.

Firth Hall, Western Bank, S10 2TN
0114 222 0468
concerts.sheffield.ac.uk

◆ Sheffield City Hall

Keep an eye out for any decent reason to get inside one of the many halls of this beautiful art-deco concert venue – particularly if it means a chance to try out your latest moves on the light-up dance floor in the Ballroom...

Barkers Pool, S1 2JA
0114 278 9789
sheffieldcityhall.co.uk

Illustration by Glenn at Eleven

The gift shops at Site Gallery and Millennium Gallery (p29) tend to be our go-to places when want to treat our friends. This bunch also never fail to satisfy:

MoonKo, by Nigel Barker

◆ MoonKo

An ever-evolving, carefully selected showcase of work by the best new designers, makers and illustrators. Jewellery, prints, t-shirts, notebooks and plates are all displayed on beautiful CNC-fabricated furniture made at Sheffield's Chop Shop, and the changing window artwork, by local illustrators like Sarah Abbott and Geo Law, is always super pretty.

89 Division Street, S1 4GE
moonko.co.uk

◆ Filibuster and Booth

Decorative brooches, vintage pearls, glimmering pendants... have a good rummage!

158 Devonshire Street, S3 7SG
0114 275 2311

◆ The Nichols Building

A two-floor treasure trove full of antiques, vintage fashions, crafts and nostalgia. Our best finds have included a lovely old Thermos picnic set, a 1940s folding table, and, for just 50p, a pristine Janet Jackson LP. Closed on Mondays.

Shalesmoor, S3 8UJ
0114 270 0798

◆ Of the Wild

Bloomin' beautiful! Flowers are always appreciated, and there's plenty to choose from in this gorgeous little shop.

10 Crookes Road, Broomhill,
S10 5BB

The Old Sweet Shop, by Nigel Barker

◆ The Framery

Lovely Tintin prints, plus the work of top Sheffield artists like James Green. Also head down the road to West End at no. 259 for some fantastic We Live Here Sheffield prints (see p32 for a peek at the artist's work).

349 Sharrow Vale Road, S11 8ZG
0114 268 1918
pictureframersinsheffield.co.uk

◆ The Old Sweet Shop

Shop and gallery space for local artists and makers located in one of Sheffield's leafiest suburbs. Prints, paintings, books and all kinds of gifts can be found in this lovely corner shop. We love the Project Trademark tote bags. Closed on Mondays & Tuesdays.

1 Nether Edge Road, S7 1RU
0114 255 8515
theoldsweetshopsheffield.co.uk

◆ The Front Parlour

This tiny vintage shop is an utter delight. Run for over 30 years by a mother and daughter duo, it's a joy to step back in time here whilst pottering around the Sharrow Vale area. Never sure of what you'll find (think 1950s handkerchiefs and nightshirts), the handwritten labels are worth a purchase alone.

Open Wed, Fri & Sat from 11am.

300 Sharrow Vale Road, S11 8ZL
0114 268 4068

The Front Parlour, by Shaun Bloodworth

Forge Bakehouse, by Shaun Bloodworth

◆ Forge Bakehouse

We defy you to walk past this place. One doughy whiff and you'll be straight through the door. We always are. Almond croissant for breakfast, a light rye loaf for lunch and some pizza dough to make tea with – sorted. And it's only a few doors down from Bragazzi's (p18), another competitor for the title of Best-Smelling Place in Sheffield.

Look out for pop-up pizzeria nights too.

232 Abbeydale Road, S7 1FL
0114 258 8987
forgebakehouse.co.uk

◆ Sharrow Marrow

As far as grocery shops go, the Sharrow Marrow, housed in what used to be a garage, is a real delight. Fruit and veg are laid out amongst curious objects: an old till here, a Bianchi bike there. There's also a cafe dishing up lunches made with stock from the shop and local butchers and bakers.

232 Sharrow Vale Road, S11 8ZH
0114 267 0133

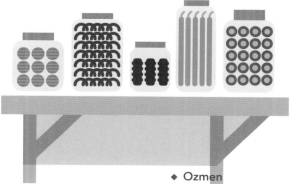

◆ Ozmen

Sticky baklava, gooey Turkish delight, imported soft drinks, loaves of moreish sesame bread baked on site, jars of every pickleable vegetable imaginable – the list of reasons to love this bright and jam-packed international supermarket just goes on and on. Seemingly open all of the time!

178-184 London Road, S2 4LT
0114 255 9411
ozmenfoodcentre.co.uk

◆ Starmore Boss

For a perfectly aged malt whisky, a cracking selection of craft beer, or a bottle of fine wine, look no further than Barry Starmore and Jefferson Boss's shop full of lovely booze. The pair also put on tasting evenings in the shop and in bars across the city – check their site for details.

257 Sharrow Vale Road, S11 8ZE
0114 453 4087
starmoreboss.com

◆ New Roots

The most charitable place to pick up your fruit and veg. New Roots, run entirely by volunteers, offers its takings – and often its food – to help refugees and asylum seekers in Sheffield. It also offers a bicycle delivery service and occasional film screenings and talks.

347 Glossop Road, S10 2HP
0114 272 1971
newroots.org.uk

◆ Porter Brook Deli

Pick 'n' mix olives and a counter full of tempting cheeses. For a perfect summer picnic, pick up supplies here and head to nearby Endcliffe Park (p55).

354 Sharrow Vale Road, S11 8ZP
porterbrookdeli.co.uk

Starmore Boss, by Nigel Barker

◆ Encore

Encore has something of a living room feel to it; it's as if you're browsing through the shelves at an old friend's house. A friend with great taste in art-house cinema, an incredible collection of badges and postcards, and a love for philosophy and music.

Don't miss this place when you're exploring the Antiques Quarter (p48) – it may be small, but we always spend ages in here, chatting with the friendly owner and discovering delight piled upon delight.

359 Abbeydale Road, S7 1FS

◆ The Last Chapter

We've treated ourselves to lovely postcards here, as well as some cracking old local history books, second-hand art tomes, and a Sheffield walking guide from the '50s. A neat and tidy little shop.

7 Rustlings Road, S11 7AA
0114 327 0341
thelastchapter.co.uk

◆ Books on the Park

The park in question is Endcliffe Park – meaning this shop is handily located for picking up materials for sunny days spent reading outdoors. A great collection of literature, local-interest pamphlets, and nonfiction – plus bargain boxes packed out front and the added bonus of folk and Americana vinyl in the back room.

Ecclesall Road, S11 8TG
0114 266 6364

BOOKS

Books on the Park, by Shaun Bloodworth

Rare and Racy, by Nigel Barker

◆ Rare and Racy

A local institution. Established in 1969, nothing much has changed in that time – and it doesn't need to. The warren of rooms house a wide range of books as well as prints both new and old (take a rifle through the folders full upstairs), paintings and a great choice of music – mainly jazz and blues.

164 Devonshire Street, S3 7SG
0114 270 1916
rareandracy.co.uk

◆ Porter Bookshop

With books upon books stacked to the ceiling and standing in precarious piles on the floor, there's plenty to keep you browsing here. All books are second-hand and all genres covered – with particular emphasis on philosophy, history and the classics. Not far from Books on the Park, The Last Chapter, and Rhyme and Reason – if you want to make a day of it.

227 Sharrow Vale Road, S11 8ZE
0114 266 7762

◆ Rhyme and Reason

A bookshop especially for children, this cute and colourful place is just as much a delight for big kids.

681 Ecclesall Road, S11 8TG
0114 266 1950
rhyme-reason.co.uk

◆ Carousel News

It's a tiny newsagent's, but Carousel manages to pack onto its shelves the city's best selection of magazines and international newspapers.

18 Division Street S1 4GF
0114 249 3326

See also:
Rude Shipyard, p14
Site Gallery, p29
Age UK, p50

The Inherited Shop, by Nigel Barker

◆ The Inherited Shop

Inherited is a gem. Its wares are carefully hand-picked, and range from locally-made jewellery to East London independent t-shirt labels. We especially love its wall of internationally sought-after trainers.

475 Glossop Road, Broomhill, S10 2QE
inheritedshop.co.uk

◆ Sakis

Penfield jackets, Norse Projects shirts and Vivienne Westwood suits – just some of the stylish sorts of names you'll find in this menswear shop. Also try Seasons, around the corner on Carver Street for lovely clothes for men and women by Joseph, Paul & Joe, Nicole Farhi, Folk and John Smedley, amongst others.

32-34 Division Street, S1 4GF
0114 303 0135
sakis.co.uk

Image courtesy of A New Shop

◆ Syd and Mallory

A boutique selling their own distinctive range of clothes made and printed by hand, as well as – upstairs in the Rag Parade – vintage menswear and curious objects of antiquity.

162 Devonshire Street, S3 7SG
sydandmallory.com

◆ CollardManson

Stylish clobber (dark and gothy), quirky shoes and shiny things galore. CollardManson bags, designed in Sheffield, are our favourite things in this artful and eclectic shop. We wouldn't mind anything from the Vivienne Westwood jewellery cabinet too!

All this and a range of lovely homewares make CollardManson extremely hard to resist.

125 Devonshire Street, S3 7SB
0114 273 7755
collardmanson.co.uk

◆ A New Shop

The bestest vintage shop in the city. A New Shop has a cracking range of pretty vintage dresses, pristine old coats, Converse pumps and ace band t-shirts. Look out for their kilo sale: £15 for a kilo of clothes – winner!

For more vintage fixes, take a look at Cow, a two minute walk away on West Street (the bright yellow shop – you can't miss it) and Freshman's on Carver Street.

25 Division Street, S1 4GE

CollardManson, by Nigel Barker

◆ Wilson Cycles

Would you rather buy a bike made on the cheap a million miles away that falls apart after a couple of years, or a handmade work of art that may well last longer than your own legs? If it's the latter, pay a visit to Nigel Wilson's Mr Ben-style shop for expert advice on all things two-wheeled.

220 City Road, S2 5HP
0114 272 3483
wilsoncycles.co.uk

◆ Cycling Emporium

Stylish shop attached to Nonnas Italian restaurant, and part of its cycling club, La Squadra. The Emporium stocks all manner of fancy bike-related gear: jerseys, Brooks saddles and bags, Rouleur magazines and, of course, strong Italian espresso.

Open Fri-Sun.

8 Hickmott Road, S11 8QF
nonnas.co.uk/cycling-emporium

◆ La Bicicleta

The bicycle equivalent of a Saville Row tailors – with lycra and carbon fibre in place of pinstripes and checks. Don't be put off though; this is Sheffield, not London, and owner Alex offers friendly, knowledgeable service to roadies and triathletes.

54 Greystones Road, S11 7BN
0114 266 2323
labicicleta.co.uk

◆ ReCycle Bikes

Up in Heeley, ReCycle refurbish donated bikes until they're good as new, and sell them on at the best rates in town. The not-for-profit organisation also trains up young apprentices in bike mechanics. Once you've got your ride sorted, look forward to free-wheeling back down the hilly road.

62-68 Thirlwell Road, S8 9TF
0114 250 7717
recyclebikes.co.uk

Cycling Emporium, by Claire at Eleven

DESIGN

Made North, by Shaun Bloodworth

ReCycle Bikes, by Nigel Barker

◆ Made North

The arrival of Made North put a collective spring in the step of every creatively-inclined bod in the city. Nestled within one of our favourite city centre buildings, the gallery and shop provides a platform for contemporary northern design in all its forms.

Look out for their changing 'Showcase' and 'Launchpad' exhibitions which focus on established designers and emerging talent.

Open Wed-Fri 12-6pm,
Sat 11:00am-4pm.

Yorkshire Artspace,
Persistence Works,
1 Brown Street, S1 2BS
madenorth.co.uk

Antiques Quarter, by Mark Howe

Sheffield Antiques Quarter is wedged between Abbeydale/Broadfield/Queens Road(s), just south of the city centre. Full to the brim with treasures, the Antiques Quarter rewards exploration, but here are our top tips to get you started...

◆ Sheffield Antiques Emporium

This palace of antiquities is perfect for losing an hour or two looking for furniture, homeware, clothes and accessories. The Emporium is also, handily, just across the road from Sheffield Antiques Centre, and at the heart of the Antiques Quarter.

Pick up a map to the quarter while you're there, and get exploring!

15 Clyde Road, S8 0YD
0114 255 0055
sheffieldantiquesemporium.webs.com

◆ Vintedge

One of the newest – and best – in the area, Vintedge has it all: an amazing selection of records courtesy of King Biscuit Time, local craft wares, a top cafe (Electric Candlelight, p9), rolls of gorgeous fabrics, and an ale shop in the form of the Hop Hideout. There's even a '50s hair salon, so you can look the part when you hang out in your freshly kitsched-out living room.

448 Abbeydale Road, S7 1FR
0114 438 0314

For more on Sheffield Antiques Quarter, and to find dates for market days and car boot sales, visit sheffieldantiquesquarter.co.uk

While you're in the area, also seek out:

Okeh Cafe, p3
Thelma's, p7
The Broadfield, p12
The Rude Shipyard, p14
Bragazzi's, p18
The Old Sweet Shop, p39
Forge Bakehouse, p40

◆ Raw Timber

Passionate about bringing old back to new, Raw Timber specialise in reclaimed timber flooring and salvaged architectural gems. Down a quiet back street close to the Antiques Quarter, their stock (mostly from schools circa 1970) includes old desks, science benches and charts explaining the rules of netball. It is the perfect place for a nostalgia-tinged rummage.

Responsible for transforming one of our favourite pubs, the York (p24), check out their site for some old-school inspiration.

150 Little London Road, S8 0UJ
0114 258 5351
rawtimber.co.uk

Raw Timber, by Nigel Barker

Record Collector, by Shaun Bloodworth, courtesy of the University of Sheffield

◆ Record Collector

Barry Everard has run this record shop since the early '80s, amassing a huge stock of over 25,000 titles on vinyl and CD both new and pre-owned. You'll be glad to see all the Sheffield musical greats represented here: Richard Hawley, ABC, Arctic Monkeys, Human League, Pulp… and you might even bump into them paying at the till.

233 Fulwood Road,
Broomhill, S10 3BA
0114 266 8493
recordcollectorsheffield.co.uk

◆ Tonearm Vinyl

The latest, very welcome addition to Sheffield's list of record shops. Tonearm caters to proper vinyl collectors with its rare 7" singles and its bunch of picture discs. We go for its Motown compilations and new releases from Sheffield bands. Generally only open on Saturday afternoons(!), but if you're in the city centre, Tonearm also stocks a number of records in MoonKo (p38).

401 South Road, Walkley S6 3TD
0114 327 1516

◆ Age UK

We're a bit reluctant to write about this place for two reasons:

1. God forbid they might get big-headed and put their prices up.

2. You might hotfoot it down there and pick up all the best buys for yourself.

You really never know what you may find here. We've faced the beautiful dilemma of choosing between an original Ghostbusters soundtrack or a New Order 7" dance remix. Other weeks have seen a toss up between Roxy Music, Joan Armatrading and the Mr Men. Great selection of books, too.

221 Fulwood Road,
Broomhill, S10 3BA
0114 268 2606

◆ The Moor Market

When Castle Market closed toward the end of 2013, we were a little worried that some of its trusty stalls wouldn't make the move over to the shiny new market on the Moor. We've been chuffed to see that most of our old favourites are all in there, though – and plenty more besides.

The market is full of locally-sourced everything – cheese, ale, bread, meat, flowers – as well as clothes, beauty stalls and places to eat. Closed on Sundays.

We do miss the Rooftop Cafe though (RIP Castle Market).

77 The Moor, S1 4PF
0114 273 5281

Other markets we like:

Nether Edge Farmers Market
Held quarterly on Sundays around the old market place, with food, crafts and live entertainment.
www.netheredge.org.uk

Bradfield Farmers Market
One Saturday a month at Bradfield Village Hall.
www.bradfieldvillagehall.org.uk

Sharrow Vale Market
Held on Sundays every few months.
www.sharrowvale.co.uk

MARKETS

The Moor Market, by Nigel Barker

Sheffield Ship Model Society at Millhouses Park, by Gemma Thorpe

PARKS

Many of Sheffield's best parks date back to the nineteenth century. They were the 'lungs of the city' at a time when Sheffielders were most in need of open green spaces where they could breathe in something a little fresher than the blackened fog of industry. Since they were often built uphill from that fog, plenty of the parks have great views, too – perfect for a summer picnic.

◆ Graves Park

J. G. Graves was one of Sheffield's most philanthropic benefactors; as well as gifting much of this park's land to the city in the 1920s and '30s, he donated money and works of art for the development of Sheffield Central Library, Graves Gallery and the Mappin Gallery (now Weston Park Museum, p64) for the good of everyone in the city. What a guy.

The public park named in his honour is the largest in Sheffield and it has it all: rolling fields, woodland valleys, ponds, a golf course, tennis courts, bowling greens, a cafe, and an animal farm.

Hemsworth Road, S8 8LL

◆ Millhouses Park

There's something for everyone at this lovely park: paddle boats, a skate park, bowling greens, an outdoor gym, rock pools, a water play area, and a cafe serving up amazing cakes.

If you're around on a Sunday, Tuesday or Thursday morning, you may be in luck to catch the Sheffield Ship Model Society navigating the boating lake with their delightful watercraft creations.

Abbeydale Road South, S7 2QQ

◆ Botanical Gardens

There is nowhere nicer to spend a relaxing afternoon in the city than this 'garden of surprise'. Extensively and lovingly restored, and continuously changing, there is always something new and lovely to look at. The pavilions are stunning, the water garden is fantastically tranquil, and the rose garden has the best choice of benches. Don't forget to seek out the bear pit.

Clarkehouse Road, S10 2LN
0114 268 6001
sbg.org.uk

Botanical Gardens, by Shaun Bloodworth, courtesy of the University of Sheffield

◆ Endcliffe Park

Queen Victoria's stern-looking statue welcomes visitors to this lovely park, opened in 1887 to mark her Golden Jubilee. Its paths lead through woodland and by streams, to duck ponds, picnic benches, a play area and a cafe (opposite, and p12). For a round walk of an hour or so, follow the Porter Brook through the park, take a look at the grinding workshop at Shepherd Wheel (one of the oldest industrial sites in the city), and head on to Forge Dam, picking up an ice-cream at their cafe before turning back.

The park is great for a bit of nature-spotting: we've spied kingfishers by the ponds and, during autumn dusk, bats swooping between the branches of the oak tree by the park's gates.

off Rustlings Road, S11 7AA

See also: Weston Park Museum, p64

Alfred Denny Museum, courtesy of the University of Sheffield

◆ Alfred Denny Museum

Housed in the University of Sheffield's Department of Animal and Plant Sciences, the Alfred Denny Museum dates back to 1905. Full of curiosities of natural history and zoology – vertebrate skeletons, huge fossils, shelves of animals preserved in jars of alcohol – this incredible place first opened to the public in 2012.

Open first Sat of each month, tours at 10am, 11am, 12pm. Free, but book in advance.

Alfred Denny Building, University of Sheffield, Western Bank, S10 2TN shef.ac.uk/alfred-denny-museum

◆ General Cemetery

Surrounded by the chirp of birds and the patter of the Porter Brook, there are few places as calming as the General Cemetery. Follow the leafy paths as they wind from the gatehouse through this bygone burial ground. Opened in 1836 to serve the growing industrial city, the land has now become a nature reserve.

Two disused chapels stand to either side of the Dissenters Wall: the neo-Gothic Anglican Chapel and the classical Nonconformist Chapel (now being developed as an arts space).

Check the site for info on upcoming tours and events.

Cemetery Avenue, S11 8NT www.gencem.org

Kelham Island Museum, courtesy of Sheffield Industrial Museums Trust

◆ Abbeydale Industrial Hamlet

Steel making on this site, right by the River Sheaf, dates back further than the 13th century. The workers' cottages, water wheel and workshops that remain were largely built in the 18th and 19th centuries. They're still in pretty good nick, and are a great place to learn all about the steelmaking processes that the city became so famed for.

Look out for the Hamlet's annual Steam Gathering, a celebration of steam complete with locomotives, vintage motors and plenty of top hats.

Abbeydale Road South, S7 2QW
0114 272 2106
simt.co.uk

◆ Kelham Island Museum

With a huge Bessemer Converter out front, you can't really miss this museum. Learn about the buffer lasses, grinders and little mesters whose work built worldwide renown for the words 'Made in Sheffield'. Admire such works of metal as the 'fancy scissors', watch the River Don Engine chug into motion and, after tea in the Little Mesters Cafe, head out to explore what else Kelham Island has to offer: architectural relics of industry and real ale (see p26).

Alma Street, S3 8RY
0114 272 2106
simt.co.uk

Abbeydale Industrial Hamlet, courtesy of Sheffield Industrial Museums Trust

NORFOLK HERITAGE TRAIL

Curious passengers pulling into Sheffield may spot a slender stone form reaching for the heavens on top of the hill behind the station. Flanked by the much-talked-about Park Hill flats, this older landmark is a mournful monument to the 402 victims of the 1835 cholera epidemic buried in a mass grave nearby. For the inquisitive, Sheffield's answer to Cleopatra's needle rewards a steep climb with a spectacular view of the city centre.

The monument is a key feature on the Norfolk Heritage Trail, a linear route which takes in the most interesting bits of the Norfolk Park area – one of Sheffield's best-kept residential secrets. The trail is best adapted to a short or long loop depending on time available. It takes in faded but still glorious Victorian mansions, rolling green parkland, ancient woodland, and some parts of the city which only a sunny day might save from being described as more shabby than chic. In Norfolk Park, the diamonds have always shone amongst the rough.

Google 'Norfolk Heritage Trail' for more info and a map of the area.

Cholera Monument illustration by Alys at Eleven. Taken from our illustrated Sheffield alphabet, which takes you on a tour of the city from A-Z, via J is for Jarvis and T is for Trams. For more see: ourfaveplaces.bigcartel.com

Don't Miss

Manor Lodge

Built around 1516, the Lodge was once at the heart of a huge deer park, and played host to a famous prisoner in the form of Mary Queen of Scots. The sprawling housing estate next door takes the shine off the historical romance, but the ruins of the Lodge are well worth a visit, as is the small visitor centre run by local regeneration heroes Green Estates.

Cholera Monument Illustration by Alys at Eleven

Jervis Lum

At the back of the charming park that gives the area its name, this beautiful wooded ravine has lain quietly undisturbed for hundreds of years, oblivious to the city which has sprouted up around it.

Wheatley's Fish & Chips

This unassuming chippy, which looks like the back of someone's house on Manor Lane, serves up some of the best fish and chips in Sheffield at prices which prove they haven't twigged that yet. Don't get your hopes up too high though – the opening hours are as old school as the pricing.

Skye Edge

Once a gathering place for would-be Chartist revolutionaries, the now-scruffy Edge is mostly frequented by dog-walkers and bored teenagers. But catch it on a fine day and you will be amazed by the flocks of homing pigeons being trained by their fanciers and by the view for miles around, stretching from the distant purple hills of the Peak District, to the industrial heartland of the Don Valley.

Words by Eric Hildrew

◆ ARCHITECTURE

Its architects, Gollins Melvin Ward, were chosen in a national competition. The brief: to design a series of modern buildings fit for the post-war influx of students, centred around a library with the capacity to hold one million volumes.

Western Bank outgrew that vision by the 21st century, but students continue to pass through the beautiful marble lobby, up the wooden stairs and past Robin Day chairs – seeking knowledge in its catalogue; losing themselves in its subterranean stacks; gazing out from the grand reading room windows, across the duck pond and leaf-strewn lawn of Weston Park. Lucky, lucky things.

Western Bank, S3 7NA

◆ Western Bank Library

A simple box form, striped with glass and stone, Western Bank Library was called 'the best modern building in Sheffield' by architecture scholar Nikolaus Pevsner. In 1959 it was opened, fittingly, by T.S. Eliot – a master of modernism in its literary form. The library holds hands with the equally modern Arts Tower via a bridge, and together they were Grade II* listed in 1993.

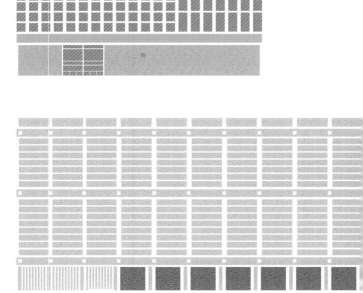

Illustrations by Glenn at Eleven

◆ Moore Street Substation

Concrete, contemporary and brutalist. Moore Street Substation lends itself to comparison with another example of post-war regeneration in Sheffield: Park Hill. Like Park Hill, the substation was built on land recently cleared of poor quality back-to-backs and, like Park Hill, it has split opinion ever since. We love it.

Designed in 1968 by Jefferson Sheard, the substation was lauded by critics; yet, despite being Grade II listed in 2013, it continues to face objection over its imposing exterior. In a prominent position along the ring road, it can't fail to catch the eye – particularly at night, when its stairwells and panels are lit up by 100,000 red, blue and yellow LEDs.

Moore Street/Hanover Way, S3 7WR

◆ Central Library

Around the entrance to this neoclassical delight are stone carvings that symbolise nine academic disciplines, all of which are represented within the building – whether in the library's collections, in its basement theatre (p35), or upstairs in the Graves Gallery (p28).

After the First World War, effort was put in to scrub-up the image of central Sheffield that had been blackened by slums and industry. Part of the plan was to create a civic centre based around a few key public buildings – including the library, which opened in 1934. Originally intended to face onto a square, the building is in fact not as eye-catching as it might have been; the rest of the square was never completed and the entrance is often shadowed by its more modern neighbours. Nonetheless, it's a beauty – especially at night when it's all lit up.

Surrey Street, S1 1XZ
0114 273 4727

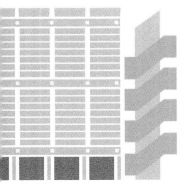

◆

Keep an eye on the online shop for our upcoming Architectural Tour of Sheffield: ourfaveplaces.bigcartel.com

◆ Sheffield Friday Night Ride

Once a month, close to a full moon, a group of like-minded people gather together and head out to explore the city on their bicycles.

Sheffield Friday Night Ride isn't a club you need to join, and it doesn't cost a penny to take part... it's a mix of cycling, fresh air, curiosity, and a chance to be sociable.

Each ride follows a theme. Past themes have included '60s Sheffield, J G Graves, sex, cemeteries, and breweries. Each ride is meticulously researched and planned and, whatever the theme, you'll be taken to corners of the city you've probably never been to before. Wherever you go, at some point there'll be an incredible view, and, being Sheffield, a really big hill to free-wheel down. The ride will end at a pub where you'll be able to wash down a beverage or two with your new cycling pals.

sfnr.org.uk

◆ Park Run

While many of us are still snoozing, every Saturday at 9am a motivated bunch of nearly 300 folk join in one of the free 5k runs around some of Sheffield's very best parks.

Park Runs are free to take part in and, if you register in advance, your time will be recorded. Great for those in training for the Sheffield Half Marathon. Check the site to find the nearest run to you and set your alarms – we'll see you at the park!

parkrun.org.uk

◆ The Climbing Works

The Climbing Works has taken the concept of indoor bouldering and exploded it for a mass market, adding illy coffee and an impeccable soundtrack of minimal techno. With acres of indoor bouldering surfaces, climbing at the Works is more like wandering around the different rooms of a super club than scratting about on brick edges in the days of yore. With stacks of easy bouldering, and a whole new wall next door dedicated to kids and beginners, the Works is the perfect place for the uninitiated to have a go.

Unit B, Centenary Works,
Little London Road, S8 0UJ
0114 250 9990
climbingworks.com

Sheffield Friday Night Ride, by Gemma Thorpe

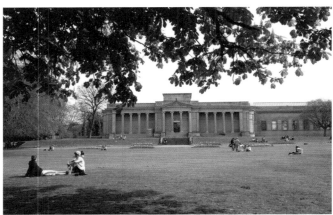

Weston Park Museum, by Shaun Bloodworth, courtesy of the University of Sheffield

◆ Weston Park Museum

With its blossom trees, duck pond and Victorian bandstand, you could spend a whole afternoon in Weston Park alone. Its local and natural history museum, though, is well worth a visit. Learn about the miners' strike, look in on the ant colony, try on a coat fit for the Arctic, and meet Snowy the polar bear.

Our favourite bit is the mock-up of a Park Hill flat, with its impassioned video defending the love-it-or-hate-it housing block, courtesy of its former caretaker – the amazingly named Grenville Squires.

Open every day.

Western Bank, S10 2TP
0114 278 2600
museums-sheffield.org.uk

◆ Abbeydale Miniature Railway

Complete with stations, level crossings, footbridges and a signal box, this charming little railway was built in the woods near Dore & Totley Station by the long-established Sheffield and District Society of Model and Experimental Engineers. Their mini steam trains run on odd Sundays and bank holidays in spring and summer – check their website for dates. All aboard!

283 Abbeydale Road South, S17 3LB
sheffieldsmee.co.uk

◆ Mayfield Alpacas

Meet the farm's funny, fleecy residents as they graze happily in the fields, and learn a little about their native Peru. You'll find the visitor centre by following the Sheffield Round Walk, or you can stop off on your way to the Peak District.

Quicksaw Farm, Fulwood Lane, Ringinglow, S10 4LH
0114 263 0033
mayfieldalpacas.com

Mayfield Alpacas, by Nigel Barker

◆ Rivelin Valley Paddling Pools

Swimming cossies on? Now get splashing! The original paddling pools were opened in 1951 and, according to a promo film from the time, were intended to be 'a source of happiness for the families of Sheffield now and in the future'. Recently refurbished with sprinklers and jets galore, they seem to be succeeding in that aim.

Open Sat-Sun and every day in summer holidays, 11am-5pm.

Rivelin Valley Road, S6 5GL

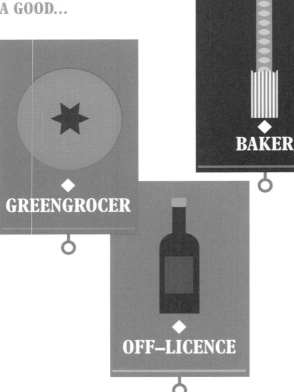

EVERYBODY NEEDS A GOOD...

BAKER

GREENGROCER

OFF–LICENCE

Beanies
Wholefood co-op with tasty treats from their Cat Lane Bakery.
205 Crookes Valley Road, S10 1BA

Fruit-a-Peel
Irresistible bags of yoghurt raisins and fizzy sweets.
279 Fulwood Road, S10 3BD

Just Natural
Olive pick 'n' mix!
209 Crookes, S10 1TE

See also: p40-41

Starmore Boss
Lovely booze, p41.
257 Sharrow Vale Road, S11 8ZE

Dram Shop
The best kind of corner shop.
21 Commonside, S10 1GA

Hop Hideout
Inside Vintedge, p48.
444 Abbeydale Road, S7 1FR

Forge Bakehouse
The best baked goods in the city, p40.
232 Abbeydale Road, S7 1FL

Seven Hills
Gorgeous if a bit pricey. Delish orange scones.
376 Sharrow Vale Road, S11 8ZP

Saxtons Home Bakery
Fresh breads baked at home and delivered to your door.
saxtonshomebakery.co.uk

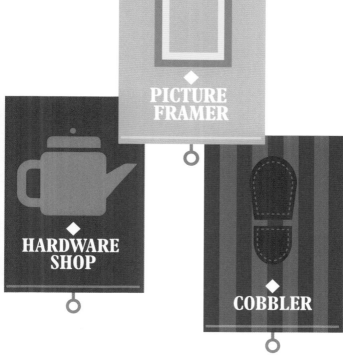

Sharrow Vale Hardware

Hardware got cool.

370 Sharrow Vale Road, S11 8ZP

Williamsons

Family-run since the 1950s.

222 Fulwood Road, S10 3BB

Bardwells

Providing electronic bits & bobs since 1945.

288 Abbeydale Road, S7 1FL

The Framery

James Green and Tintin! See p39.

349 Sharrow Vale Road, S11 8ZG

West End Picture Framing

We Live Here prints and quality framing.

259 Sharrow Vale Road, S11 8ZE

Momento

Cheap and cheerful – but good quality.

15 Shortridge Street, S9 3SH

Robinsons

Cheerful and speedy repairs.

415 Ecclesall Road, S11 8PG

Charles Brooks

Repairs and lots of top quality men's shoes too: Loake, Grenson and Trickers.

245 Fulwood Road, S10 3BA

Illustrations by Glenn at Eleven

◆ Hathersage Swimming Pool

Open-air swimming amidst the glorious scenery of the Peak District – really, what could be nicer? Don't be deterred if it's a bit chilly out, the pool is heated to an almost balmy 29°c.

Hathersage is a lovely Peak District village to spend the day in. After a swim, head to the main street for a potter around the shops and tearooms, finishing off at the brilliant David Mellor museum and shop. There's a regular bus from Sheffield to Hathersage (no. 272), or you can catch the train (it takes about 20 minutes).

Open late March-September – see website for times.

Oddfellows Road,
Hathersage, S32 1DU
01433 650843
hathersageswimmingpool.co.uk

Hathersage Pool, by Kathryn at Eleven

David Mellor Design Museum, by Nigel Barker

◆ David Mellor Design Museum, Country Shop and Cafe

David Mellor, Royal Designer for Industry, has an international reputation as a designer, manufacturer and shopkeeper. We feel incredibly lucky to have this place on our doorstep.

The museum, cafe, factory and shop showcase the designs of Sheffield-born David Mellor (1930-2009) and his son Corin, alongside a well-chosen selection of homewares.

The Round Building (the award-winning circular cutlery factory) is open for viewing, and on weekdays visitors can usually see David Mellor cutlery being made.

In the 1950s and 60s David Mellor designed a series of street lamps, bus shelters, benches, and litter bins – these outdoor pieces of furniture are now on display in the Street Scene leading up to the shop. Traffic lights (designed by David in 1966) never looked so beautiful.

Round Building, Hathersage, S32 1BA
01433 650220
davidmellordesign.com

◆ Chatsworth House

Gardens, fountains, sculpture, animals, a maze, ice-cream, a historic house – don't miss any of it. One of the country's best-known and well-loved estates, Chatsworth is approx 20 minutes by car from central Sheffield. Immortalised on TV and in film, Chatsworth attracts thousands of visitors each year and, although we go often, we never tire of pottering round this stunning place.

The gardens are transformed every September and October by the contemporary sculpture exhibition Beyond Limits – that's our favourite time to visit.

A visit to the farm shop is a must – follow the signs from the house.

Bakewell DE45 1PP
01246 565300
chatsworth.org

The maze at Chatsworth, by Glenn at Eleven

Curbar Edge (above), and Jolly's (below), by Glenn at Eleven

Keen to explore more of the Peaks? Of course you are! Well, you're in luck – the OFP Peak District book is coming soon...

◆ Jolly's

We were beyond giddy the first time we met Louis, the Vintage Citroen van parked up at Curbar Edge. Homemade cakes and warming drinks at the start/end point of one of our favourite Peak District walks – winner! Guaranteed to make you smile after a wind-blasted walk along the Edge.

Most weekends, 10am-6pm (4pm in Winter)

Curbar Edge Car Park,
Hope Valley, Curbar, S32 3YR

Yorkshire Sculpture Park, by John at Eleven

◆ Yorkshire Sculpture Park

Approximately half an hour up the M1, YSP is an extraordinary place. Over 500 acres of parkland and a number of indoor galleries house changing exhibitions of contemporary sculpture. Recent artists have included Joan Miró, David Nash and Yinka Shonibare. Permanent works by Antony Gormley, Barbara Hepworth, James Turrell (don't miss the Skyspace) and Henry Moore are scattered across the beautiful landscape.

West Bretton, Wakefield, WF4 4LG
01924 832631
ysp.co.uk

◆ Hepworth Wakefield

Ten minutes in the car from YSP, this striking gallery, designed by architect David Chipperfield, further enhances Yorkshire's reputation as a national centre for sculpture. With a comprehensive collection of work by Barbara Hepworth, as well as painting and sculpture by her modernist peers, it's fantastic to have this place on our doorstep.

There is an ongoing programme of contemporary work, while further galleries feature a fascinating insight into Hepworth's processes and materials.

Gallery Walk, Wakefield, WF1 5AW
01924 247360
hepworthwakefield.org

Hepworth Wakefield, by John at Eleven

Bike Show at the Civic, by Nigel Barker

◆ The Civic

We heart the Civic. Where else in Yorkshire could you see a European art-house film in the morning, a Design Museum travelling exhibition in the afternoon, and comedy or theatre by night? Take a look at the Civic's website, there's usually something interesting on – especially in the Gallery.

Only 25 minutes by train from Sheffield.

Hanson Street, Barnsley, S70 2HZ
01226 327000
barnsleycivic.co.uk

◆ Yorkshire Wildlife Park

In early 2010 the so-called Lion Express landed in nearby Robin Hood Airport, and the park's main attraction had arrived in town: 13 lions, saved from poor conditions in a Romanian Zoo. Walk through the park's many acres and you'll come across zebras, lemurs, tigers, baboons and meerkats, too. Yorkshire Wildlife Park has also set up a foundation to support the conservation of endangered species in the wild.

off Warning Tongue Lane,
Doncaster, DN4 6TB
01302 535057
yorkshirewildlifepark.co.uk

FESTIVALS & EVENTS

Sheffield Zine Fest
sheffieldzinefest.wordpress.com

Sheffield Adventure Film Festival
shaff.co.uk

Sharrow Lantern Carnival
creativeaction.net

Sheffield Food Festival
sheffieldfoodfestival.org

Doc/Fest
sheffdocfest.com

Sheffield Design Week
sheffielddesignweek.co.uk

Sheffield Pride
sheffieldpride.co.uk

Sheffield Children's Festival
sheffieldchildrensfestival.co.uk

Sheffield Grand Prix
sheffieldgrandprix.co.uk

Tramlines
tramlines.org.uk

Eid Festival in the Park
sheffieldheritage.org/eid

Sheffield Fayre
norfolk-park.com

Sensoria
sensoria.org.uk

Festival of the Mind (biennial)
festivalofthemind.group.shef.ac.uk

Off the Shelf
welcometosheffield.co.uk/visit/
off-the-shelf

Art Sheffield (biennial)
artsheffield.org

Yorkshire Artspace Open Studios
artspace.org.uk

Sheffield Print Fair
sheffieldprintmakers.com

**Kelham Island Victorian
Christmas Market**
simt.co.uk

MORE

◆ Further listening

You could start with Def Leppard (if that's your bag), before taking an '80s detour via The Human League, Heaven 17, ABC and Cabaret Voltaire. Pulp epitomise '90s Sheffield, and Richard Hawley's Coles Corner is a modern classic. The Arctic Monkeys, meanwhile, are busy making it big in the US. If you want to discover the latest Sheffield bands then delve into the Drowned in Sheffield column on drownedinsound.com. Whatever you do, don't forget John Shuttleworth – especially the classic *Two Margarines*.

◆ Further viewing

For Sheffield-made thrillers, try *A Daring Daylight Burglary* – from 1903, it's action-packed at just five minutes in length – or *Threads*. Be warned: the latter, with its scenes of the city in nuclear peril (complete with panic-stricken shoppers on the Moor) is as traumatising today as it was when it first aired in 1984.

No doubt you're already familiar The Full Monty. If you're after something with a better soundtrack, take a look at Eve Wood's documentaries on Sheffield's music scene in the '80s and '90s: *Made in Sheffield* and *The Beat is the Law*. Film company Warp formed on our doorstep, meaning much of their output is great for a game of spot-the-Sheffield-landmark (Kebabish in *Four Lions*, Park Hill in *This is England '86*, etc).

◆ Further reading

In *The Road to Wigan Pier* George Orwell wrote of how ugly and smelly he found industrial Sheffield in the 1930s; we'd like to think he wouldn't have so strong an adverse reaction if he could visit again today. John Betjeman, meanwhile, granted the city a little more majesty in his 1967 poem *An Edwardian Sunday, Broomhill, Sheffield*.

For more recent Sheffield-based literary exploits, see: the *Sheffield Anthology*, *Now Then* magazine, and Hallam Uni's annual creative writing publication *Matter*.

◆ Sleeping

As we live in Sheffield we don't have much cause to frequent its hotels. But there are some lovely places to stay – from hotels to suit all budgets in and around the city centre, to picturesque B&Bs, hostels and campsites out in the Peak District.

Take a look at airbnb.co.uk, tripadvisor.co.uk and welcometosheffield.co.uk/stay

We'll have more info on places to sleep on our website soon.

◆ ABOUT US

We are Eleven. Our Favourite Places is a self-initiated project by our studio. We are a team of designers, writers and illustrators based in Sheffield. We created (just about*) everything you see in these pages.

We created OFP to celebrate Sheffield and encourage people to visit our hilly home city. So far we've published three OFP guide books, made a short film, devised a series of walking tours and created an online city guide. In short, we've been busy.

Words: Kathryn Hall, Claire Thornley
Design: Claire Thornley
Illustration: Glenn Thornley, John Gelder, Alys Mordecai

elevendesign.co.uk

◆

*We've had lots of help with Our Favourite Places this past year and we'd like to say a massive thanks to our contributors, who've not only helped with this book but also kept the OFP site afloat! BIG thanks to: Iain Broome, Jacqueline Chell, Sarah Cockburn, Jane Faram, Eric Hildrew, Joanne Mateer and Greg Povey.

We're lucky to work with some super talented photographers too. Nigel Barker, Gemma Thorpe, and Shaun Bloodworth have taken fantastic images for us, and their work makes a HUGE difference to OFP. For more see:

> nigelbarkerphotography.co.uk
> gemmathorpe.com
> shaunbloodworth.com

All images are credited, and we'd like to thank everyone for allowing us to use their images.